THE STENDAHL
HAMLET SCENARIOS

Borgo Press Books Edited or Translated by FRANK J. MORLOCK

THE STENDHAL
HAMLET SCENARIOS

AND OTHER SHAKESPEAREAN SHORTS
FROM THE FRENCH

Edited and Translated by

Frank J. Morlock

THE BORGO PRESS

An Imprint of Wildside Press LLC

MMX

CONTENTS

DEDICATION

To

WILLIAM SHAKESPEARE

Whose works have continued over the centuries to not only maintain their beauty but to inspire beautiful works from others. If these translations do not embellish your works, may they at least lead to a greater understanding of the magnitude and impact those works have had on succeeding generations everywhere.

And to

TITANIA,

My Fairy Queen

You know who you are!

INTRODUCTION

Stendhal (the pen name of Marie-Henri Beyle) 1783-1842, is best known today as the author of the novels, *The Red and the Black* and *The Charterhouse of Parma*. His clearheaded analysis and romantic feeling, his use of irony and psychology, are extremely modern, and served as a precursor of Romanticism in France. His youthful (he was then nineteen) attempts to rewrite *Hamlet* are interesting in many respects. First of all, he intensifies the conflict by making Ophelia the daughter of Claudius. He also varies the action in several ways, and even plans to move the scene of the action to Warsaw under King Boleslas (a substitute for Claudius). Although these several attempts were abandoned, Stendhal demonstrates a real dramatic sense and a bold willingness to modify the Shakespearean original—and at the same time proving how powerful these stories were and how subject to variation.

Auguste Vacquerie (1819-1895) was related through his brother to Victor Hugo by marriage. He wrote several plays on his own, and also collaborated with Paul Meurice. He was a journalist of republican conviction and went into exile with Hugo. *Falstaff: The Tavern Scene* (published in

1895, but probably written much earlier) was a verse re-write of the same scene in Shakespeare's *Henry IV Part I*. It does not really improve on the original, but does demonstrate the continued French fascination with this material. I've translated it into prose, the verse being unmemorable.

Louis (Lucas) Gallet (1835-1898) was a prolific librettist and often worked with Massenet. *Titania* was published five years after his death in 1903. This beautiful little musical drama demonstrates the continued influence of Shakespeare even at the end of the nineteenth century. Gallet also worked on *Ascanio* (derived from Dumas and Meurice's *Benvenuto Cellini*), which in my opinion is the most beautiful work I've ever translated. I did *Titania* in free verse and I think it holds up very well.

Georges Ephraim Mikhael (1866-1890) was a poet and playwright, apparently of the Symbolist school. *Le Cor fleuri*, here translated as *Oberon's Horn*, moves away from Shakespeare's direct influence, but indicates how a great original work can create new patterns in much later writers, like a stone thrown in a pond that produces ever-more-distant ripples. I like it almost as much as *Titania*, and also translated it into free verse.

Paul Meurice (1818-1905) had a long and distinguished career as a dramatist collaborating with Dumas, Sand, and Hugo, as well as writing many plays on his own. A graduate of Charlemagne College, he was introduced by Charles Vacquerie to Victor Hugo in 1836 and became his acolyte. He was also on friendly terms with Alexandre Dumas *Père*. He must have been a fairly good diplomat to remain on speaking terms with two men who were often at odds from professional jealousy.

With Dumas he collaborated on *Hamlet* (1848), *The Two Dianas* (both the novel and play), and *Benvenuto Cellini* (1852). The *Cellini* later became the basis for the libretto of the Saint-Saens opera of the same name. Dumas regarded Meurice as something of a raffish, happy-go-lucky type. Considering that Dumas was regarded by most as rather wild himself, this indicates that Meurice must have been lively company, to say the least.

Supposedly, Meurice asked Dumas to lend him 30,000 Francs so that he could make a dazzling, advantageous marriage. Dumas was willing, but, as he told Meurice, "You know I don't have one-twentieth of that sum." "But your signature is worth more than 30,000 francs on a new manuscript." "Yes, but unfortunately, I don't have a new manuscript on hand." Whereupon Meurice extracted from a box he had with him the text for *The Two Dianas* in novel form. Dumas thought about it and said, "Leave that here, and come back tomorrow." The next day Meurice had his money and presumably got the girl. Jules Janin told this story to the Goncourts, and Paul Foucher, Victor Hugo's brother-in-law, retold a similar version in his memoirs.

For this reason, it has been long argued that Dumas never wrote *The Two Dianas*, although it was published with his works. It has been pointed out that Dumas denied having written the book, but that was when *The Two Dianas* was being made into a play, and Dumas was in trouble with his creditors. Meurice paid Dumas *Père*'s share to his son, Alexandre Dumas, *Fils*. It seems unlikely he would have given Dumas a share if he'd not had a hand in the play and the novel on which it was based.

Meurice was a staunch Republican, and wound up spending ten months in prison in 1848 for printing an article on the right of asylum in his newspaper, *L'Evenement*, by Charles Victor Hugo, Victor Hugo's son. In 1869 he was a cofounder of the journal *Rappel*, which published literary and theatrical criticism. There he worked with the young Émile Zola.

In addition to his beautiful Dumas adaptation, *Ninety-Three*, Meurice adapted Hugo's *Les Miserables* and *Notre Dame de Paris*. All three plays are very faithful and powerful dramatic works. He also collaborated with Georges Sand on the dramatization of *Cadio*. Meurice also wrote a *Falstaff* (adapted from the tavern scene in Henry IV, Part 1), *Antigone*, *Fan Fan Le Tulipe*, and several less familiar titles such as *Paris*. In 1896 he published, as editor, *The Love Letters of Victor Hugo*.

Between 1880-85 Meurice essentially directed the publication of Hugo's collected works. As Hugo's literary executor, Meurice set up the Victor Hugo museum in the Place de Vosges. He wrote several plays without collaborators, including *The Lawyer of the Poor* (1856), and three novels, *La Famille Aubry* (1856), *Les Chevaliers de l'Esprit* (1869), and *Le Songe de l'Amour* (1869)

Meurice also worked on three other Shakespeare adaptations—*Falstaff*, *Hamlet* (with Dumas), and *The Dream of a Summer Night*.

The anonymous *French Lear* (*The Beggar King* in French) was a play produced at fairs in the nineteenth century and even into the early twentieth. Perhaps to satisfy a simple sense of justice, Lear regains his throne. But the play is powerful, sardonic, and well motivated psychologically, despite some changes from the original model.

These plays indicate both the interest the French playwrights demonstrated in Shakespeare's dramas, and their tendency to rework his material into semi-classical forms, slimming it down and going for the essentials. Studying these works expands both our understanding of the French reaction to Shakespeare—and also of Shakespeare himself. Often we think that a Shakespearean play can only be told the way Shakespeare told it; here we see that there are a myriad of alternatives.

The plays collected here precede and postdate The Romantic Revolution in France, which was triggered by the appearance of the English Players in 1828, when Macready and Miss Smithson stunned Paris audiences by actually acting Shakespeare. (The French tradition was for tragedies to be declaimed rather than acted.) Full-length Shakespeare adaptations were written by Alexandre Dumas *Père* (*Hamlet, Romeo and Juliet*) by Vigny (*Othello, Shylock*) by Sand (*As You Like it*), to mention only the best known works.

Dumas and the other Romantic writers insisted that reworking Shakespeare's dramas was the most transforming experience in their artistic lives, and influenced them heavily thereafter.

—Frank J. Morlock
San Miguel de Allende, México
November 2009

THE STENDAHL HAMLET SCENARIOS

by

Stendhal

CAST OF CHARACTERS

KING CLAUDIUS
HAMLET
QUEEN GERTRUDE
GENERAL CASIMIR
OPHELIA
A SERVING GIRL

PLAN FOR *HAMLET* (1802)

ACT I

Claudius tells Casimir why he made him come from the army. Hamlet and Gertrude enter. Gertrude is coming to be present at the farewells of the King and Hamlet.

Hamlet, Gertrude

Gertrude makes efforts to extract Hamlet's secret from him. Hamlet displays chagrin that she has so soon given a successor to his father, Ophelia arrives unexpectedly. Gertrude leaves her with Hamlet, after begging her to tear his secret out of him.

Ophelia, Hamlet

Development of the love of Hamlet and Ophelia. Hamlet makes her swear to keep an inviolable secret and confesses that his father[1] has appeared to him and ordered him to avenge his death but without naming his assassins.

---

[1] His "brother" in text.

ACT II

Hamlet comes on stage beside himself. His father has just appeared to him and ordered him not to leave Elsinore without punishing his assassin, Claudius.

Hamlet, Ophelia

Ophelia comes on stage attracted by the screams of Hamlet. At the sight of her, Hamlet's despair redoubles. He makes her repeat her oath and confesses to her the frightful truth. Ophelia despairs. She defends her father with all the warmth of filial love and that which she has for Hamlet.

Claudius, Hamlet, Ophelia

The King arrives and orders Hamlet to leave. Hamlet declares to him that important interests keep him at Elsinore. The king gets carried away and orders him to leave. Hamlet leaves, threatening him in a double entendre reply.

Ophelia, Claudius

The King engages Ophelia to restore her young lover to duty. He notices an appearance of violent agitation in her.

Claudius (alone)

No longer doubts that Hamlet is conspiring against him. He determines to cause him to perish in some way or other.

CASIMIR enters

Casimir comes to testify to his surprise that Hamlet doesn't want to leave. The King tells him that the time has come for Hamlet to die. He is perplexed as to the means. Casimir advises him to poison him at a meal. Claudius consents to it.

ACT III

Hamlet expresses his troubles and the means he has taken to avenge his father. He waits for his mother who has summoned him.

Hamlet, Gertrude

Gertrude comes on behalf of the King to invite Hamlet to the meal at which the King intends to poison him. Hamlet makes his mother admit her crime, makes her share the order of his father who orders her to give herself up completely to her own remorse. She tells her son that she intends to retire to a convent in the realm of the Czar, her brother. That she will confess her crime there and find a means for him to mount the throne of his ancestors. It's agreed that Hamlet will help her escape in two hours.

Hamlet leaves.

Gertrude, Claudius

Claudius comes to inform himself of the success of Gertrude's mission. She announces that Hamlet refuses.

She exposes her remorse to the King. (Gertrude exits.)

Ophelia, Claudius

Ophelia comes to tell her father that she fears for his life and begs him to abandon a crown which exposes him ceaselessly. She obtains nothing. She leaves.

Claudius

Alone, Claudius resolves to make Hamlet perish as soon as possible.

ACT IV

Hamlet's despair. He considers if he must give up his life. He concludes he cannot until his father is avenged. He waits for Ophelia who has asked him for a final meeting.

Hamlet, Ophelia

She arrives. The scene contains major developments. She does everything to dissuade Hamlet from his project, doesn't succeed and leaves in final despair.

Hamlet

Hamlet is in despair. He goes to prepare, his friends to come carry off his mother and then march against Claudius.

ACT V

Claudius is on stage. A servant girl comes to tell him that his daughter is dead and to bring him a letter she wrote before stabbing herself to death. "Watch out for a hand that was dear to you." The serving girl leaves.

Claudius (alone)

He sees the horror that is spreading around him. He has a moment of remorse, but he overcomes it and resolves to kill the Queen. He enters into her apartment. He kills her. At the moment he is leaving he meets Hamlet and his troops. Hamlet is recognized as King. He orders that Claudius be led off to prison. A serving girl of Ophelia brings him a letter she wrote dying. His despair.

They come to announce that the independent commoners have massacred Claudius. He restores liberty to Denmark and kills himself.

END OF THE TRAGEDY

Claudius discovers the conspiracy of Hamlet in the third

act. He locks up Ophelia and declares to Hamlet that if he doesn't remove his partisans from Elsinore he will stab Ophelia to death.

HAMLET, VERSION II
27 BRUMAIRE XI (18 NOV. 1802)

ACT I

Crimes, however they may be hidden, sooner or later are discovered and punished.

Everything must give way to duty, even love.

CAST OF CHARACTERS

BOLESLAS, King of Denmark
HAMLET, son of Alfred, nephew of Claudius
REGANE, mother of Hamlet, widow of Alfred, wife of Claudius
OPHELIA, daughter of Claudius
CASIMIR, general of Claudius' army

The scene is in Poland at ___.

PROLOGUE

Alfred, great Prince and great law giver, reigned in Denmark. This great prince had formed the plan of giving Denmark some of the institutions of more southern nations that he thought useful for the happiness of mankind. He began some of his reforms and didn't hide the most important that he intended to make from his retinue. Thus he attracted the hate of the high nobility of his kingdom and the clergy.

Alfred had a brother named Claudius, a greedy and brutal genius, profoundly ambitious. He had made himself famous in war under the reign of his father, Christian. He bore with impatience the distance from affairs that the wise Alfred kept him, until the discontent of the nobles made him give birth to the plan of dethroning the King, his brother, and taking his place. He raised the standard of revolt with the great men of the kingdom and assembled an army. Alfred marched against him, vanquished him, and pardoned him. The perfidious Claudius accepted the pardon but never abandoned his design. He counted on finding a suitable means sooner or later. He spent a year in this expectation at his brother's court.

During this time, Alfred, instructed by his brother's revolt, did much to conciliate the nobles and the priests. Claudius saw with terror the number of malcontents diminish and finally recognized that a rebellion would never place him on the throne of Denmark. Immediately his course was taken: subjugate the Queen, poison the King, get himself named Guardian of young Hamlet, cause him to perish and finally reign. Such were his projects. He was handsome, in the flower of age, had previously shone in tournaments. He reconciled to the court, feigned a return to the tastes of earlier years, and was amiable. The Queen was a woman; she loved him.

Soon she sacrificed to him all her duties; their secret relationship lasted a year. Claudius, persuaded her that Alfred knew about it and intended to cause both their deaths in horrible torments. Finally, he murdered him with her consent. The Queen was named guardian of her son. After two months given to propriety, Claudius married the Queen and trouble stirred up causing the Estates to assemble and name him King. Bring all this to the laws and customs of Poland where the action takes place.

Alfred had named Hamlet his successor, but Claudius having stirred up trouble and on the pretext of Hamlet's youth had himself named King by the magnates.

CAST OF CHARACTERS

Claudius, ambitious in every sense of the term, and consequently as great a scoundrel as it is possible to be.

Hamlet, a young man of the greatest courage and the noblest frankness. He had seen war under his father; he's twenty-two-years old. Desperately in love with Ophelia, pursued by the ghost of his father.

Gertrude, guilty wife and full of remorse, loving and fearing her son, she hates Claudius but doesn't dare show it.

Ophelia, young and charming princess, adoring her lover and loving her father.

Casimir, fine general, an instrument of Claudius, acid brained.

PLAN

Hamlet is a lover who avenges his father by killing the father of his mistress.

ACT I

The King explains to Casimir for what purpose he's recalled the army to Elsinore. Gertrude and Hamlet enter. The King says his goodbyes to the prince. Hamlet remains alone with Ophelia who conjures him to confess his secret to her. His struggles. Finally he admits that his father has appeared to him and ordered him to avenge his death on his murderers. But he doesn't name them to her.

ACT II

Hamlet comes on stage beside himself; his father has just appeared to him and ordered him to avenge him on Claudius who murdered him with the agreement of the Queen. Ophelia, drawn by his cries comes on stage. Hamlet makes her swear to keep the secret and reveals what he's just learned. She suspects the veracity of the apparition. Hamlet describes it to her. Ophelia defends her father with all the warmth of the love she has for Hamlet and that she bears to her father. Casimir comes to press Hamlet to leave. The prince charges him to tell the King he cannot yet do so. Casimir displays his astonishment. The King arrives and Hamlet repeats the same thing to him. The King is very astonished and orders him to leave. Hamlet exits. Claudius remains alone with Casimir attesting that the suspicions delaying Hamlet make him apprehensive and end by making him determined to cause him to perish that very day whatever may be the means.

ACT III

[none]

ACT IV

Hamlet's despair. He deliberates whether he can give up his life. He concludes he cannot so long as his father is not avenged. He awaits Ophelia who has insisted on a last meeting. She does everything in the world to dissuade Hamlet from his project, doesn't succeed and leaves in the last despair. Hamlet forms a conspiracy against Claudius. At the moment he is most animated the King sends to tell him that he consents to give him his daughter in marriage, that all is ready and that they are waiting for him. In consternation, Hamlet refuses.

ACT V

They announce the madness of Ophelia. Scene between her and Hamlet where she is mad from love. The King comes. He has a moment of remorse at the sight of all the misfortunes which surround him, but he overcomes it. He determines to kill Gertrude. He enters the Queen's apartment. Hamlet arrives with his confederates. The King leaves covered with Gertrude's blood. The confederates kill him. Hamlet learns of the death of Ophelia; Hamlet kills himself after having disposed of the crown.

The scene is in Poland in the days of high chivalry.

* * * * * * *

I intend to depict in the tragedy of Hamlet the opposition of filial love and love.

The protagonist is Hamlet
after him Ophelia
then Claudius
Finally Gertrude.
Casimir, the tool.

After the prologue, what is needed to begin the first act of Hamlet?

ACT I

To discover the murderers of his father, punish them, marry Ophelia, reign, and since Claudius reigns in Denmark to do great deeds in war and found a kingdom.

Ophelia? To marry Hamlet and to find supreme happiness in her possession.

Gertrude. To protect Hamlet from the traps Claudius may be setting for him, and to avoid being suspected by

Claudius? To reign peacefully over Denmark and in order to do this to cause Hamlet to perish without being suspected of his death.

Who are the characters most necessary for the exposition?

1. Claudius and Casimir. This scene about what Hamlet wants. To take his last orders from Claudius, to say his goodbyes to Ophelia and to leave for the army.

Ophelia? To see her lover before his departure and to obtain the secret of the cause of his melancholy.

Gertrude? To watch over her son's well being, to penetrate the reasons that cause Claudius to give him the command of his army and to give advice to Hamlet on the way of conducting himself.

After that:

2. Hamlet comes with his mother to take leave of Claudius. The scene over, what does Hamlet want? To see Ophelia and leave.

Claudius? That Hamlet leave promptly so as to be the sooner defeated.

Ophelia? To see her lover.

Gertrude? To discover the secret of the sadness of her son so as to be able to guide him more securely.

Casimir? To leave promptly; to cause Hamlet to perish and to regain command of his army the soonest.

3. Gertrude, alone with her son, presses him to unveil his secret and does not obtain it. She calls on Ophelia to tear his secret from him, Hamlet. She leaves her with him.

That scene over, what's Hamlet want? To say his farewells to Ophelia.

Gertrude? That Ophelia discover Hamlet's secret.

Ophelia to discover her lover's secret and to say farewell to him.

Claudius and Casimir, idem.

4. Ophelia remains alone with her lover to conjure him, to learn from him the cause of his melancholy. He resists for some time, finally he gives in. He makes her swear to keep the secret and tells her that his father, Alfred, has appeared to him and ordered him to avenge him. He did not tell him the name of his murderers. He's leaving for the army with the intention of abandoning a court where he no longer has any friends and to discover the murderers of his father. They develop their love and leave.

ACT II

What does Hamlet want after the last scene of the first act? To depart.

Ophelia? To see her victorious lover again soon.

Gertrude: To see Ophelia and learn Hamlet's secret.

Claudius and Casimir, *idem.*

Alfred appears to Hamlet, telling him the names of his murderers: Claudius and the Queen, and ordering him to avenge him before leaving. He orders him to leave Gertrude to her own remorse.

1. Hamlet comes on stage, beside himself. He develops his horror through interspersed phrases.

After this scene, what's Hamlet want? To avenge his father by causing Claudius to perish.

2. The shouts of Hamlet attract Ophelia. She arrives, sees the trouble of her lover, conjures him to tell her the cause. Hamlet makes her renew her oath and tells her. She employs all means to dissuade Hamlet from his design which is to avenge his father. Hamlet leaves, determined to avenge him.

What is Ophelia's determination? To prevent Hamlet from avenging Alfred.

3. She is trying to figure out a way when Gertrude comes to learn if she has succeeded with her son.

What must Gertrude do? Everything in the world to learn

Hamlet's secret from Ophelia.

What must Ophelia do? Have a horror of Gertrude.

What must Hamlet do? Run to the friends of his father, reveal to them the secret of his death and excite them to extort vengeance with him.

4. Gertrude asks Ophelia what Hamlet's secret is. Ophelia has a horror of her and displays it with interspersed phrases, and she leaves.

What makes Ophelia flee? The horror Gertrude inspires in her.

5. Short monologue of Gertrude's horror. She sees the day of vengeance approaching. It was in vain she thought the Gods were appeased. She sees Claudius.

How does Gertrude behave at the sight of Claudius? Her first sensation is one of terror. After Claudius announces what brought him, she tries to excuse her son.

What drives Claudius? The desire to make Hamlet leave and to know what is keeping him.

6. He asks Gertrude what's retaining Hamlet at Warsaw. He tells her that he's just ordered that he be found and that they tell him what the King demands of him.

Gertrude allows her suspicions to break out. Claudius repulses them with scorn and bitterness.

After this scene what does Claudius want? To make Hamlet leave.

What does Gertrude want? To excuse her son and watch over him.

What must Hamlet want summoned by Claudius? To hide the horror and hate which inspires him. But he can only partially do so.

7. Hamlet arrives. Claudius asks him the reasons for his delay. Hamlet develops his pride, the King, his haughtiness. He orders him to leave. He tells Gertrude to leave with her son and to make an effort to calm him.

What is Hamlet's interest? Seeing that....

13 BRUMAIRE XI
(4 DECEMBER 1802)

Hamlet is pursued by the shade of his father to whom he cedes (sacrifices) his love.

ACT I

Claudius reveals the subject to Casimir. Interview between the King and Hamlet. Confidences from Hamlet to Ophelia. Gift of the scarf. The lovers' farewells.

ACT II

The apparition of Alfred before Hamlet. Scene between the latter and Ophelia. The King comes to reiterate the order to leave; he leaves in a rage. Gertrude arrives, Ophelia leaves.

Scene between Hamlet and his mother in which the latter confesses her crimes and names Claudius as her accomplice. They agree that Hamlet will, that very evening, cause his mother's escape. Hamlet leaves to find the means to avenge his father.

ACT III

Hamlet is on the stage. Ophelia comes and asks him on whom he must avenge the death of his father: on Claudius.

A wrenching scene between the two lovers. Hamlet consents to take no action until Ophelia has seen her father. Hamlet leaves, Claudius arrives.

Scene between Ophelia and Claudius. He remains inflexible. Ophelia leaves, desperate. Casimir arrives. The King tells him that he no longer doubts that Hamlet is conspiring. He orders him to go seek a body of troops that he's brought to Warsaw. Meanwhile, he's going to try to lure Hamlet to a place where he can be sure of him. "He loves my daughter; I have my snares completely prepared. If he gives in, he's dead."

ACT IV

Scene between Hamlet and Gertrude. Claudius has proposed to give his daughter to Hamlet. (Boleslas announces to Hamlet that he is giving him his daughter and that his presence is necessary with the army. Everything must be done right away.)

Hamlet wants nothing better, but again, he fights this wish. He fears to offend his father. His mother, moved by reasons of politics, ends by persuading him. He finally agrees that she may go announce his consent to the King. She leaves.

Hamlet remains alone in a moment of joy, but soon remorse agitates him. His father appears to him; he shows him his wound with a look of reproach.

"He's showing me his wound. Oh, I read my duty in it."

He decides to avenge his father. At that moment Ophelia comes to find him.

"Come dear Hamlet, they cannot wait for you any longer."

Hamlet refuses. Ophelia at first is beside herself. Then her despair intensifies. She leaves in a deep stupor.

An envoy of the notables comes to announce to Hamlet that everything is ready, and that he can no longer hang back without ruining them.

Hamlet leaves determined on the most prompt vengeance.

ACT V

Claudius is on stage. They come to tell him of the madness of his daughter. He has remorse but overcomes it. He goes to the Queen's rooms to kill her.

Hamlet enters to save his mother. He sees Claudius coming from her rooms with a bloody dagger. He kills him.

Ophelia arrives mad. Wrenching scene between Ophelia and Hamlet. She notices the body of her father. Reason returns to her.

"Ah, I recognize him, and my dream is accomplished."

She kills herself.

Hamlet: "You won't be alone long in the tomb."

He returns the government to the notables, advises Poland to create a republic and kills himself.

If I keep the situation with the dagger, Ophelia cannot be more crazy.

She could still be in presenting the dagger to Gertrude but this situation doesn't enter fully into the character of the tragedy.

ACT I

SCENE 1

Claudius, Casimir.

CLAUDIUS: Finally, in Elsinore, I see Casimir again. And you are going to give me news of my army.

CASIMIR: Milord, I have taken it to the border and without the unexpected order which recalled me to you, perhaps the Swedes would already be vanquished.

CLAUDIUS: That order astonishes you? Don't think, dear Casimir, you've lost the confidence of your king, and be sure, since he recalls you here, that he has something of greater importance to confide to you than the spaces where you command the army.

CASIMIR: Lord, I submit with respect to the orders that you are pleased to give me. Still, if I were allowed to speak, I would say that the rumor of my disgrace is disseminated everywhere and Prince Hamlet, who, they say, will command the army, would have reason to fear me if my love for my prince did not assure me of his favor.

CASIMIR: They told you true, Casimir, and Hamlet will command the army; you will be his lieutenant; but don't be frightened; it's there you will render me the greatest service you could possibly render me, and you will finally calm the malaise which never ceases to agitate me. You think, without doubt, that happy Claudius, brought by your efforts to the throne of Denmark, has no further desires. But you know that I mounted it by what vulgar imbeciles call crimes, and that so long as there remains a single witness, my crown is not safe on my head. Already, the imbecile Gertrude who tires me with her endless, vain remorse, would have gone by now to join her spouse in Hell if I weren't afraid of giving substance, through her death, to the dark rumor which accuses me of the death of Alfred. What encourages the partisans of my brother, is this young Hamlet who, although so young, knows how to conquer the love of the people. They complain his youth is deprived of his father's crown. They complain Alfred was carried off in the flower of his age. You know what limits I set to his life; I don't think it necessary to describe them further. But for some time this so lovable prince, that only seemed occupied with war games, has become sad and pensive; he repulses all my advances with a somber coldness. I thought even one day to surprise a look full of fury which he cast at me. I thought that his troubles came from love which, as you know, united him to my Ophelia from the tenderest age. But what do I divine when I learn from that frank and candid soul that she is suffering as much as I am from Hamlet's melancholy, and she doesn't know the cause better herself? Then my suspicions became complete. I had him summoned and in the presence of his mother, with all the friendship that a tender uncle has for a nephew, I asked him the cause of his habitual melancholy. I spoke to him of the crown that I was keeping for him on deposit, I called him my son and wanted to embrace him, but he escaped from my arms with horror and seemed dismayed by a terrible spectacle. His terrified mother called him; he seemed to soften at her voice, he went to her, then he seemed possessed by an even greater horror and left in terror. Then I no longer doubted anything. He knows that his mother knifed his father; he knows that it was I who provoked the crime. I resolved on his death, but it was necessary that she determine the manner to divert all suspicion. I sent you the order to break off negotiations broached with the King of Sweden; I nominated him as general of my army. You are his lieutenant. I am going to receive his farewell here in an instant. You will leave tonight. You will reach the army day after tomorrow. You will give battle. One of your archers will deliver me from my enemy and happy Claudius will have nothing more to do than to reward his loyal Casimir.

* * * * * * *

ABANDONED SITUATION

Hamlet seeing Boleslas' dagger raised against his mother, Regane, and threatening to stab her if he doesn't withdraw. "O gods, in this terrifying moment, either bend or dictate your wishes to me."

Bad verse but very expressive of a feeling.

Thoughts for the characters.

Boleslas, ambitious in the full meaning of the word. It follows naturally from that, that he must bear a mortal hatred to Hamlet.

Thoughts on the dialogue.

Gertrude (name to be changed) I can no longer bear these places which remind me of my spouse and my crime.

Situation.

Claudius knowing that Hamlet intends to avenge his father on him, and not having sufficient troops to defend himself, seizes his mother, Gertrude, and says:

"Dare to avenge your father and I will cut your mother!"

Gertrude exhorts her son to vengeance and kills herself.

* * * * * * *

Claudius, knowing that Hamlet adores Ophelia, and not having enough troops to defend himself, exposes himself to Hamlet holding a raised dagger over Ophelia.

"Go on, avenge your father."

This situation seems good to me because it's in the spirit of the play, presenting the opposition between love and filial love.

THE GHOST: (to Hamlet) I was murdered by Gertrude and her accomplice, that only you may appoint his punishment, avenge me on him.

Hamlet, in the farewell scene with Ophelia, speaks of the love of the notables for him and the ease he would have had in troubling the State, if his love had not held him back.

BOLESLAS, holding a dagger to the breast of Ophelia: "Well! avenge your father. Leave Warsaw and Poland, instantly and alone, or it's all over with her life."

HAMLET: Oh, gods in this terrible moment, either bend or dictate your wishes to me.

CLAUDIUS [change the name of Claudius to that of Boleslas]: Well! By what right do you pretend to my love, guilty woman? Since you betrayed your first husband who will answer to me for your word?

CLAUDIUS: Every moment that he lives is stolen from my life.

BOLESLAS: But who's been able to hurry Hamlet so? I am sure that only yesterday he was not conspiring. How has he been able to choose the moment when I shall crown his intentions?

HAMLET: Since my father has charged me with his vengeance I no longer know myself. I don't want any more indifference. A secret furor animates me. I feel myself being carried away; I'm thirsty for the blood of Boleslas.

PLAN

In this play I intend to depict the conflict between filial love and love.

Hamlet is pursued by the shade of his father to whom he gives up his love.

[The last plan for the play has been abandoned because I found in the 5th Act of *Hypermnestra* the situation of mine which I had taken from The Memoirs of a man of quality—H. Beyle.]

The scene is in Poland in the times of High Chivalry, which furnishes me with a tint of love and honor whose effect will be most touching.

Boleslas
Regane
Hamlet
Ophelia
Casimir.

ACT I

SCENE 1

Boleslas exposes the subject to Casimir, his general: he treats him as an intimate (literally "tutoyer's him). Interview between the King and Hamlet in the presence of Regane.

Confidence by Hamlet to Ophelia. Gift of the scarf. Farewell of the lovers.

ACT II

Alfred's apparition appears to Hamlet. Scene between the latter and Ophelia. The King comes to reiterate to Hamlet the order to leave. He leaves in a rage. Regane arrives. Ophelia leaves.

Scene between Hamlet and Regane in which the latter confesses her crime, and names Boleslas as her accomplice. They agree that Hamlet will come that evening to help his mother escape.

Hamlet leaves to devise a means to avenge his father. (These means will be announced in that which precedes.)

ACT III

Hamlet is on stage. Ophelia comes and asks him on whom he must avenge the death of his father: On Boleslas. Wrenching scene between the two lovers. Hamlet consents to do nothing until Ophelia has seen her father. Hamlet leaves. Boleslas arrives.

Scene between Ophelia and her father. He remains inflexible. Ophelia leaves desperate. Casimir arrives. The King tells him he no longer doubts that Hamlet is conspiring. He orders him to go find a corps of troops to be brought to Warsaw. While waiting, he's going to try to entice Hamlet into a place where he can be sure of him. "He loves my daughter. I have my snares all ready. If he gives in he is dead. He adores my daughter. I'll tell him I want to reward his love before he leaves for the army, and that tonight I intend to celebrate his marriage in the chapel of my castle. If he comes there, I'll have him arrested."

ACT IV

Boleslas, alone, is uneasy. The refusal Hamlet has given his daughter convinces him more and more that he is conspiring against him. One of his officers comes to report that all is quiet. He goes over his dispositions for defense and is ready to withdraw, when they come to announce to him that his castle is surrounded by troops. They come to announce to him that the attack has begun; he sends an officer to observe it. A moment later, an officer comes to tell him the first has been killed. That all his suspicions were well founded, that Hamlet is advancing at the head of the conspirators, that the whole city is declared for him.

Boleslas says, without being understood, two words to his officer.

ACT V

HAMLET: (alone) They've made me give in. In an hour I am marrying Ophelia. My mother has convinced me, but will you be satisfied, shade of my father? (Remorse; apparition—his father points to his wound with a look of reproach.) He's showing me his wound. Ah! I read my duty in it. (He determines to avenge his father. At this moment Ophelia comes to find him.)

OPHELIA: Come, dear Hamlet; they can't wait for you any longer.

(Hamlet refuses. Ophelia flies into a rage at first. Finally, her despair intensifies. She leaves in a profound stupor. Hamlet leaves, determined on the most prompt vengeance.)

This apparition in the 4th act is excellent in that it reconnects Hamlet to his father's vengeance in a manner such that he can no longer recoil.

BOLESLAS: Go find my daughter.

(After a few moments Ophelia arrives:

OPHELIA: What do you want, father?

BOLESLAS: In this danger your place is beside me.

(Hamlet rushes on him)

HAMLET: Die scoundrel!

(Boleslas turns and lets him see Ophelia.)

BOLESLAS: If you approach she is dead. Make your accomplices leave.

(they leave) Leave Warsaw alone and instantly or it's over with her life. Give me your word of honor you won't call your friends.

HAMLET: I give it.

BOLESLAS: I leave you five minutes alone with her. Decide for yourself. See if you wish to sacrifice your mistress to the crown. (he leaves)

New and very tragic scene.

17 FRIMAIRE XI
8 DECEMBER 1802

I am abandoning this subject which may furnish one of the most beautiful tragedies of the French theatre. But it's not forever that I leave my dear Hamlet; at least, I hope not.

I am abandoning it because the situation in the 5th Act is in *Hypermnestra* and I don't want to make my debut with a copy.

I found in that play the character of Boleslas, totally ambitious to develop. A character of whom Acomat is but a part. For Boleslas is in the first plan and the principal actor of the tragedy.

No confidants.

A superb and very natural exposition. All the systems of chivalry to develop.

Pity in the scenes between Hamlet and Ophelia; terror in those with the ghost and finally the struggle between filial love and love. Primary passions of man that every spectator has experienced.

I can treat this subject with great success six years from now, by which time I will be sure of my style. Then I will bury *Hypermnestra* or I will fall. It will be necessary if one cannot show Ophelia mad.

The situation is in nature. It remains to foresee the effect it will produce. One must have experience and style to dare to risk it on the stage.

There was one King, Boleslas II, King of Poland and tyrant to whom I can relate this tragedy. I had the plan to render Regane interesting and to make her appear much less. Boleslas must kill her in the 5th Act.

I read Alfieri and I am very satisfied. I've read the letters of Clement to Voltaire which didn't seem very judicious to me. I am determined to make my debut with *The Amorous Philosopher*.

H. Beyle.

3 Prairial XI
23 May 1803

To begin my Hamlet with
Leave me, horrible spectre, etc.

FALSTAFF: THE TAVERN SCENE

by

Auguste Vacquerie & Paul Meurice

(1905)

CAST OF CHARACTERS

FALSTAFF
HENRY, PRINCE OF WALES
POINS
GADSHILL
PETO
BARDOLPH
FRANCIS, THE WAITER
THE HOSTESS

FALSTAFF: THE TAVERN SCENARIO

A room in a tavern. Tables, crockery, glasses.

NIGHT

AT RISE, the Hostess and Francis are on stage. Gales of laughter outside.

HOSTESS: Finally! God be praised! There are my good apostles.

(Enter the Prince and Poins laughing. They are half masked. Poins is carrying a little box which seems heavy enough.) The Prince and Poins! Masked and alone! Where are the others?

POINS: They are coming.

HOSTESS: But why these masks?

POINS: A little joke.

HOSTESS: One day, one of those jokes will get their man

hanged. Pillaging travelers!

PRINCE: Not so, my good woman. No, pillaging pillagers!

HOSTESS: (to Poins) Really?

POINS: Yes, on my soul! We left Jack with his three robbers to attack travelers without us at night. But hardly had he stolen off with the fat sum, then we fell on him and robbed the fat man.

PRINCE: Poins, hide the coffer. That gold, you know, will be restored without it being missed. (Poins leaves for a moment with the box and the masks.)

HOSTESS: But Falstaff?

PRINCE: (laughing) You should have seen him in his delirium, running away and cursing. Ah! God! How he made me laugh.

POINS: (returning) And when we listen to the poltroon, the braggart, trumpeting the exploits of his valor to us,— (shouts of distress outside) It's them.

BARDOLPH: (running in impetuously) Help! Oh! The Prince!

GADSHILL: (also running in) Worthy hostess, hide me! God! Milord!

PETO: (also running in) Robbers!— His Highness!

BARDOLPH: (to the hostess, low, pointing to the Prince) Was he laughing when he came in?

HOSTESS: He was laughing, brave Henry!

BARDOLPH: (to Gadshill) The Prince laughed.

GADSHILL: (to Peto) The Prince laughed.

PETO: (looking for a fourth that he doesn't find, to himself) The Prince laughed.

HOSTESS: But Sir John? Where did you leave him?

GADSHILL: In the field, sweating, roaring, wheezing.

PETO: He's not long winded.

VOICE OF FALSTAFF: (outside) Massacre!

POINS: (low to Prince) There he is! Some self control. We're going to laugh.

(Enter Falstaff. He arrives running and all out of breath. Stops short seeing the Prince, places his sword and buckler on the table, then falls into a chair, breathing hard.)

POINS: Good evening, Jack! Where are you coming from?

FALSTAFF: (without looking at him, fuming and grumbling) Curse the cowards! Let them all go to the Devil! Amen!— Waiter, my glass of sherry.

(Francis takes a huge goblet from a counter and pours a whole bottle into it. Falstaff takes it and empties it.)

FALSTAFF: Infamous life! Oh, if I were to persevere in it! No, rather stick it up, resole it, or even mend it. Eh! Didn't you hear me, my clown? Cursed be all cowards! A glass of sherry.

(Francis hurriedly brings a second bottle, pours it in the goblet and Falstaff drinks again.)

FALSTAFF: Is there no manhood left on earth?

PRINCE: (to Poins) Have you ever seen a cask like that?

FALSTAFF: (to Francis, drinking this time in a gulp) Ah, I taste the lime in this wine. This corrupted century is only a knavish trick. All the more, I hate cowardice that adulterates the wine. The cowards, the rogues. Go your ways, old Jack, and die when you like. If valor hasn't left the earth, I'm a kippered herring! Are there three brave men in England spared by the envious gibbet? No, and one of those three is fat and growing old. God help us. Down here one only sees baseness. Cursed be cowards. I say it without cease. (drinking)

PRINCE: Hey! Old bowling ball! Ah, indeed! What's

making you croak?

FALSTAFF: (rising) Who? You, the son of a king! But I intend to expel you from your estates, my dear fellow, with no more than a broadsword! Why, I pretend to hunt, under your eyes, with my staff or until my last hair of my head is shorn, like a flock of geese, all your people ruined! Prince of Wales, you!

PRINCE: Say what, fat paunch!

FALSTAFF: Coward! Aren't you? And this Poins?

POINS: (hand on his dagger) Sack of wool! You call me coward! I'm going to exterminate you!

FALSTAFF: (jumping back) Me, call you coward? I will be damned before I call you coward! Only, wise guys, you shove people aside to show them your shoulders. That's very witty. (to Francis) Some sherry, then. If I've drunk today, I am a rogue.

(The waiter brings a third bottle.)

PRINCE: Two empty bottles, and your chin is all running, goose.

FALSTAFF: Bah! Bah! (drinking) Again, I say, cursed be all cowards.

PRINCE: Why, what's it all about?

FALSTAFF: (excitedly) What's it about? I, Falstaff, Bardolph, Peto, Gadshill, we had in our hands a thousand guineas tonight.

PRINCE: Where are they, Falstaff?

FALSTAFF: Alas! Re-stolen. A hundred bandits came—

PRINCE: A hundred—?

FALSTAFF: May I be hanged if I didn't fence, myself, alone, with a dozen at least, for two hours. I escaped by a miracle or I intend that you die. Count.

(pointing to his breeches) Here! Four blows, twelve in my doublet. My breeches crushed. See, I'm not lying to you.

(pointing to his sword all notched) My sword, a saw. Ecce signum. In short, I never did better since I became a man. Wasted heroism! Cursed be all cowards.

(pointing to his companions) Hal, question them! If those thieves lie, they are all children of Hell! traitors—

PRINCE: (to Bardolph and the others) Yes, my masters, tell us about the carrying off, a little.

BARDOLPH: (with embarrassment, consulting Falstaff with a glance) The four of us, being fallen on—a dozen horsemen—

FALSTAFF: Sixteen at least, milord!

GADSHILL: We tied them up

PETO: Heavens! I didn't see all that!

FALSTAFF: Brute! Will you shut up! All were gagged, all tied to the ground. All! All! Or I am no more than a Jew! A Hebrew Jew.

BARDOLPH: Then, as we were sharing the loot, six or seven came—

FALSTAFF: (warming up) Who let loose the others. Still others came. They fell on us.

PRINCE: Eh! What! They all charged you in a cowardly way—

FALSTAFF: All! Hal, I don't understand what you mean by all? I had, for my part, fifty of the bravest. Fifty! Or I'm only a boot of turnips! Yes, surely, they were really fifty-two or three who attacked your old Jack at one time, and slashed at him until he let them have it. If I lie to you, I am—I am nothing but a biped!

POINS: God grant that he didn't kill one of them.

FALSTAFF: That wish comes too late, for I peppered two. Alas! Yes, I am afraid two of them got their pay. Two rogues in, Buckram. If I am telling you a tale, spit on me, call me your horse. You know my parry, in which I am without rival. Well, there I was, holding my blade thus, when four rascals in Buckram—

PRINCE: Four? By our lady, you only said two?

FALSTAFF: Four Hal, no offense.

POINS: Yes, four, he said four.

FALSTAFF: (acting it out) Then, from the front, then. But, without troubling myself by their joint attacks, I had blocked their seven points with my buckler—

PRINCE: Seven? No, four.

FALSTAFF: In Buckram I say.

POINS: Yes, four in Buckram?

FALSTAFF: Seven! Seven! With my sword!

PRINCE: (low to Poins) Eh! The courage of a coward. You will see the seven will gradually grow in number.

FALSTAFF: Are you with me, Hal?

PRINCE: Very much so.

FALSTAFF: The thing is worth the trouble. Then, these nine in Buckram—

PRINCE: (to Poins) Good! Two more already.

FALSTAFF: (miming a ferocious fight) They began to break, yelling Jesus! But as for me, I hacked them to pieces. Implacable as bronze. How many dead? Let's count? Horrible. Seven to eleven!

PRINCE: Eleven grown from two! You see us astounded.

FALSTAFF: But the Devil was in it! Three dirty dogs, dressed in light green, traitorously took me from behind. For it was dead failure, this murderous night. One couldn't see one's belly.

PRINCE: (rising) Oh, the brazen liar! Tell me, how could you clearly prove that these men were in light or dark color, if you couldn't see your belly in this shadow? Huh! Answer! What can you tell us now?

POINS: Your proofs! your proofs!

FALSTAFF: (majestic) What! By force? Never! Go, threaten me with irons, with torture. Force can get nothing from me. That's my nature. Give you my reasons, by force? Proofs in number equal to the mulberry bushes. But, nothing will tear proofs from me by constraint!

PRINCE: (rising) Ah, my patience encourages impudent tales much too long. This boastful coward, who everywhere breaks beds and horses, this mass of flesh—

FALSTAFF: Avaunt! Eel skin! Scourge! Bow string! Perch! Stockfish! Needle!

(stops, coughing) But for this damned asthma, I would speak to my hearts content.— Alder tree! Spindle! Scabbard! Tax collector's measure!

PRINCE: There! Very well! Breathe a bit, then start again. March to the end of the ignoble litany. But first of all, a single word.

POINS: Jack, hear this.

PRINCE: Yes, we saw you, Poins and I, you four, fall on two old travelers, scoundrels, then steal their gold. Now see, in a breath, your lies crumble before the truth. At that moment, I threw myself on you four, together with Poins, and that in your drunken face, without striking a blow, we took back the loot. And we have it still. What's more, it is here. And you, Falstaff, running and shouting. Oh, oh. With the bellows of an enchained bull, you saved your paunch. Mustn't you be a fat rascal, to have broken your sword coming here, so as to support the story of your glory? Well, lie again! Find a way out. Piece together, if you can, your tattered honor!

POINS: Yes; get yourself out of that, my old friend, Sir Jack. Let's see you do it!

FALSTAFF: (shrugging his shoulders) Then you think I don't know how to recognize you? As well as he who engendered you, my master! Would you like to see the heir apparent killed, my legitimate Prince? Oh! Fie! By me, puny one? You know quite well, I am as valiant as Hercules. But instinct was there, whispering to me: recoil! Lions always respect royal blood. I was afraid, but from honest and fair instinct, wanted to cover us forever with praise and esteem. For myself, a generous lion. For you, legitimate Prince. Ah, indeed! You've really recovered their ransom, my dear boys, my chums, hearts of gold, brave lads? Let's amuse ourselves, have a blast. Oh! Harebrained youth. Would you improvise a comedy!

PRINCE: Title: save yourself if you can! Right, heart of stone?

FALSTAFF: Henry, do you want to shame me? Let's leave that. You know, my son, that a reprimand by the King awaits you tomorrow. Is your response prepared?

PRINCE: My word, no! But here, catechize me. I am the scolded, you the scolder. Be the King.

FALSTAFF: The King? Me! That's easy.

(he makes a sign, they put an armchair on the table and help him to mount it) This chair is my throne. This spit, my scepter. And here's my crown.

(They pass him the spit and a round holder used for holding bottles)

(All laugh.)

FALSTAFF: Yes, laugh. If grace has some spark left in you yet, you will all be moved. There! Some sherry!

(Francis brings a fourth bottle and pours it in the goblet.)

Needed to light my eyes and put a paternal tremor in my voice.

(he drinks)

PRINCE: Here's my bow.

FALSTAFF: And here's my oration.

HOSTESS: How funny he is.

FALSTAFF: (softly) My Queen, come—moan lower.

(on a signal, Francis has improvised a banner from a dish cloth) Form ranks, my nobility, around my banner.

HOSTESS: A true monarch.

FALSTAFF: Silence, beer bottle! And the rest of you, silence, also! I am speaking here as the father, as the King. My son, you are my son, at least I hope so, and believe it. Besides, for proof of conjugal fidelity, I have your horrible tic and your beastly underlip. My son, then, you live ill, surrounded by good for nothings, tramps and ruffians.

PRINCE: Father, I admit it.

FALSTAFF: Still, it struck me, at your side, I've seen a virtuous man whose name escapes me.

PRINCE: (stupefied) A virtuous man, father! Really? What man is that, if it please Your Majesty?

FALSTAFF: Why, an imposing man, my word, of firmness, bright eyes, gracious manner, noble bearing! About fifty—thereabouts. My God, perhaps, indeed, sixty. To hide nothing from you. Ah, I have it now, he's named Falstaff. Well, yes, if debauchery has fallen on this man. But, no, no, virtue speaks and shines in his eye. And if the tree is recognized by its fruit, my son, as the fruit by the tree, then I repeat, the skin of this Falstaff contains an honest man. Kick out all your bandits, but cherish him always. Now, what have you been doing these last five days?

PRINCE: A King speak like this! This vulgar fellow exasperates me! Come down from there. I shall take the role of my father.

FALSTAFF: You dethrone me! So be it!

(they help him down) Loan to royalty the quarter of my amplitude and my majesty, and you can later hang me by my paws like a gutted rabbit.

PRINCE: The humble heart!

FALSTAFF: Are you ready?

PRINCE: I am ready.

(The Prince easily clambers into the chair.)

FALSTAFF: Everyone judge, my masters.

PRINCE: Ah, there you are, Henry. Where are you coming from?

FALSTAFF: From the cabaret, Milord.

PRINCE: There are terrible grievances laid on your account.

FALSTAFF: God's blood! They're telling you tales. The young prince—go, go, he's fine and able to defend himself.

PRINCE: What! You swear, impious child! In the future don't raise your eyes to me. I renounce you. You are going straight to Hell. You take for your companion a demon in the features of a fat old man. Your friend, your Pylades is an ambulatory hogshead. How can you suffer that warped horror, that debauchee with grey hair, that toothless infamy? What's he know? To puke and drink sherry. To cut a slice of bread and swallow it down. What is his only talent? Trickery. What trickery? That does ill and abuses all good. Perverse in what? In everything. Laudable in what? In nothing.

FALSTAFF: Not so fast, Milord! I'm not following you very well. Of whom is Your Grace speaking?

PRINCE: Of that old libertine, of that voracious hog, of that Falstaff.

FALSTAFF: (as if stupefied) Falstaff! I know the man, yes.

PRINCE: Really?

FALSTAFF: But to add that I know in him more faults than in myself, that I reject. That he is old—his grayness perhaps accuses him, and I pity him. But that he is either a greedy-guts or briber, I boldly say no before all, Milord. If to sugar Spanish wine is a crime, God save sinners! If he tumbles into the abyss to be jovial, who will pardon? If because one is fat, one is condemned, then we must, to demonstrate integrity like Lord Pharo, boast of thin cows. No, no. Kick out Bardolph, Peto, the insolent Poins. But leave me with Falstaff, the loveable, excellent, pure, sweet, great hero that all admire, And much more than a hero, he is what he is, Sire. My good Jack, exiled by your perverse son, would be the Sun banished from the universe.

PRINCE: (coming down from the chair bowing and laughing) Conclusion. Sun, must you be adored?

FALSTAFF: (rising modestly) Oh, I only call myself the Sun by a simple metaphor. First of all, the Sun itself is not divine. For that reason, my boys, he needs wine for his divinity. Ah, wine! I'm very thirsty. Come on. Have 'em pour me some.

(The waiter brings a fifth bottle and the goblet. Falstaff rejects the goblet and drinks from the bottle.) Yes, this is the other Sun, whose gleam bowls us over, which one mustn't worship by half. There it is—wine, friend and savior. Young, I languished—liver arid and pale, that, as is known, only denotes the male. Wine revived me with its foaming philter. It's to wine that I owe all this charming wit which pours from my mouth where the salt of Greece abounds. A cup of the most sparkling words in the world. Hal, you haven't let stagnate in you the frozen blood transmitted by your father, the King. But like terrain that's sterile and dull, you warm yourself up with our huge bumpers. And you leave, refreshed by emptied flagons. Ah, if I had a thousand sons I would think to do enough for them, and I would hold their souls sufficiently instructed if, as a rule of conduct, I inculcated into them on this earth, where no step is safe, the horror of colored water, and the love of pure wine! For wine will make man passionate, proud and brave. Everything in this world is only filthy, and it's wine that cleanses.

(drinking from the bottle in great gulps)

PRINCE: (laughing) Good! Drink, it's clear that after this hymn to wine, that, the better to cleanse yourself, you're going to drink without end.

FALSTAFF: (pulling the bottle from his mouth.) I don't drink! I believe Epictetus said, "Wine is milk for the old." I don't drink, I nurse."

(he takes his feeding bottle and suckles greedily.)

CURTAIN

TITANIA: A MUSICAL DRAMA

by

Lucas Gallet & André Cormeau

1903

CAST OF CHARACTERS

TITANIA, Queen of the Fairies

HERMIONE

ROBIN, Bastard son of Oberon, an elf

OBERON, King of the Fairies

MATHIAS, a shepherd.

ACT I

IN THE FOREST

A clearing in an ancient forest. Under the oak of the fairies young girls dance to the sound of a rustic orchestra. The old shepherd Mathias passes amongst them stopping at one group then the next. Robin teases the girls who are dancing.

MATHIAS:

Go dance beneath the green oak
Dance under the oak
While the day is bright
And the fountain is visible.

ROBIN:

When the owls hoot at midnight
Blonde Titania passes by
Leading the hunt.

MATHIAS:

And the game she pursues
Is neither doe nor hind
It's some handsome libertine of the night.
Dance beneath the green oak
Dance under the oak

ROBIN:

The crazy wife of Oberon
Is only beneficent in broad day light.
But formidable in the house of night.
Bad luck to the one who comes sitting
By himself under the black oak's bows.
Dance under the oak while day is bright.
And the fountain is visible.

(Night comes on bit by bit. The voices of Mathias, Robin
and the Chorus reply to each other alternatively, as the
composer directs.)

ROBIN, CHORUS, MATHIAS:

With how much care you guard a sheep from the wolf.
Guard, guard, with a jealous eye,
Your lovers round about you!
Titania, the blonde
Ensnares with her eyes,
And with her golden hair enchains,
And drags you away.

While day is bright
Dance under the oak.
Robin, Oberon's bastard
Can tell about it; he knows all about it
In his pranks.
To her spouse, the king of elves,
Each morning she recounts
Her fantasies
And the king doesn't always laugh!
But from the vine of mad love affairs
The Queen imbibes pleasure.
And passes
When the owls hoot out midnight
Leading the hunt.
The sky is black, the oak is black
Don't you see her
In the depth of the woods down there?
Titania! Titania!

(Frightened, screaming, the girls disperse and flee, Robin, satisfied with having frightened them, follows them laughing. The shepherd Mathias leaves in his turn, with a slower step, murmuring some scraps of the preceding ballad. The stage remains empty for a moment. The last faint gleams of golden light hiding in the tree tops go to sleep. Yaun appears, a dreamer seemingly in ecstasy.)

YAUN:

O green mossy freshness
O dying rays of day

O shivering stars
How beneficent and sweet this hour
To dream and love.
Love, an old word that comes to the lips.
Love, an eternal deception.
Love, which does harm.
No, it's not you that I am calling to.
It's to maternal nature
That cradles me in its powerful arms.
Nature that laughs in marvelous flowers,
And sings in streams.
Nature at once wild and caressing.
Nature with a thousand secrets
Attracts me, entrains me
Into the silence of the forests
Far from human deception.
Always further, always higher
On the wings of my dream.
I will keep going, I will sing.
Forever alone beneath immense heaven
Until the august and sacred day
When all is finished, when all begins.

(Hermine appears, a bit hesitantly. As soon as she sees Yaun, she comes toward him and calls him.)

HERMINE:

Yaun.

YAUN:

Hermine!

HERMINE:

Where are you going with such a slow step
And with eyes full of dreams?

YAUN:

Down there. Into the night. I dunno.

HERMINE:

What are you looking for?

YAUN:

Some vague poem.
The alluring chimera which always flees us.

HERMINE:

That's the monster I've been told of
Who seduces quickly, but who kills.
Stay among us. From childhood
We have lived together
And our future was the same.
I love you, and I know you love me.
Very tenderly, like a sister

Let's taste that sweetness once again.
While I am knitting white wool
I will listen to your beautiful poems.
In the humble hours of our ancestors
I will weep over your sadness
And laugh with your songs of joy.

YAUN:

O dear sister, nothing more than my sister.
Yes, I love your ingenuous soul
And memories are dear to me
Of our carefree childhood.
I want you to be happy
But that you cannot be with me.
An invincible attraction pulls me
Far from men, toward the unknown.
I will only be a creature of misfortune
If I remain captive of earthly things.

HERMINE: (anguished)

You will never love?

YAUN:

I don't want to love.

HERMINE:

O cruel word.

YAUN:

Hermine, goodbye!

HERMINE:

I dedicated my life to you,
Yaun, tenderly, humbly.

YAUN:

You will suffer through me. Go, dear girl,
Pure as your name which speaks your purity.
Your angelic heart and your heavenly grace,
At his hearth he'll make a place for you.

HERMINE:

No other will have me; I no longer belong to me!
Go your way, poor soul!
Go! Someday you will weep.
Intact, I will have kept the treasure of your tenderness
Disdained today.
With a resigned heart, I will offer you
In advance, submission to my destiny.
G'bye!

(she distances herself rapidly)

YAUN: (watching her go, pensively)

Sweet child! Ah, if I knew how to love.
But, vainly this word love always oppresses me.
I will never love; At least, I will not love
Anything—unless it is, under heaven, an ineffable love
Unalterable,
A love that knows
Only eternal spring.
That's never touched by the outrage of Time.
A wife, always beautiful in her splendid youth
A heart always ardent in magnificent passion
No fleshly miseries
Ideal tenderness and eternal intoxication.

(to himself, laughing bitterly)

Poet! Madman! Shut up! Striding toward infinity
In the immense desert of men and things.

(Night has come enveloping the distant forest in shadows.
Yaun stretches out on the heath under the oak of the fairies. Soon a pure white moon rises through the branches
and the thickets, inundating the clearing with its rays. A
distant horn sounds. Imprecise voices sing around Yaun,
who rises up, surprised. The hoots of owls reply to each
other through the leaves. Far away, very distant, a clock
tolls the twelves strokes of midnight. The acorns of the
oak are illuminated. A supernatural sheen is added to the
moonlight. Scenic symphony. Mimicry by Yaun of what is
going to come.

(Titania roars in, in a burst of light. At the sight of Titania Yaun instinctively utters a great scream and recoils before her. Then he speaks to her as she looks at him silently, smiling, enigmatic.)

YAUN:

Your light feet, your rosy feet
Beflower without touching
The soil, all bathed with light.
And your face with haughty grace
Dazzles my humble glance.
Your eyes are more brilliant than the evening star
Who then are you, nocturnal huntress?
Woman, goddess, or fairy?
Tell me.

TITANIA:

Woman, always beautiful in her splendid youth
Heart ever ardent in magnificent passion
No fleshly miseries
Ideal tenderness and ideal intoxication
That's the way you were talking just now.

YAUN:

Then you heard me?

TITANIA:

Through shadows and space
I hear, I see.

YAUN:

Titania!

TITANIA: (smiling, agreeing)

You've got my name right.

YAUN:

And it's you, the immortal
You, the unalterable beauty
You that I evoked in my dream.
You, chimera and yet reality.
I love you.

TITANIA:

And just now,
You were disdaining love.

YAUN:

I'm ignorant of it, still
Leave for me your golden hair
Spread on your white shoulder.

Extend your cool arms to my embrace,
Burn me with the fire of your eyes
Be without pride, be pitying
Of a wretched being
Who weeps at your feet.

TITANIA:

On Earth, where we are, I cannot love.
Still, I will love you if you like
With a love more powerful than that of men.
Follow me, Yaun, come into my palace
Into the mysterious domain
Where Oberon rules, and I am Queen
Where by my whim and my will
If I were to love you here, I'd become mortal
At that very moment I would lose my beauty.
Yaun, give me your life and your soul:
In exchange, I will give you changeless love
And unending sensuality.

YAUN:

Let me be nothing, let me be annihilated
Beneath your glance and in your arm!
Carry me away, take me!
Let's forget everything in delight.
I adore you.

TITANIA:

O poet, o king!
Let's leave for the country of ecstasy.
Spirits of the shadows surround us!
Errand boys with gigantic wings
Carry us off, forever united
Into infinite space.

(At Titania's voice, a horse, white like foam from the sea, roars from the woods. Wings of light beat at his flanks. Titania and Yaun mount together, bestriding the chimera and disappear. Triumphal music.)

CURTAIN

ACT II

THE REALM OF OBERON AND TITANIA

The fairy kingdom of Oberon. Lying amongst his favorites Oberon caresses the hair of Philida, who is stretched out beside him. In the midst of a great calm voices rise in space. Impression of beatific sensuality.

VOICES IN SPACE:

Night and day! Day and night!
Everywhere light
Time, on a light wing
Flies!
Kissing on the lips
Entwined couples
Slowly pass.
And in baskets
Of odiferous flowers
Rest worn out
Elves, leprechauns
And laughing fairies
As Oberon

Slowly caresses
The long golden hair
Of his Philida,
In his arms, swooning.
And through the woods
Titania, amorous huntress,
Still wanders.

OBERON:

Sound, music of birds,
Song of elves, murmur of breezes
Crystalline voices of streams!
Be an invisible orchestra. And you dance
O my beauty of a day, O blonde Philida
Dance!

(laughing)

And if I doze off during the concert
Frolic quietly on your naked feet.
And leave me alone in my sweet sleep.

(Philida rises lazily and begins to dance to the music of an invisible orchestra. Around her, fairies in languishing poses. Little by little Oberon dozes off. Philida's dance continues. The dancer, finger on her lips, distances herself. The other fairies follow her. All vanish. Oberon naps. A short symphony, at its termination Robin appears. He comes, light of foot, gay of air, mockingly, and remains for a moment, motionless, contemplating the napping

Oberon.)

ROBIN:

He's sleeping like a common spouse
While far from him
Titania is preparing a vexatious jest on him.
That's enough sleep, illustrious papa
I have more care of Your Majesty than you do.

(Robin brushes Oberon's face with a flower he holds in his hand.)

OBERON: (half waking)

Hey! Who's waking me? Who dares?
You my Queen?

ROBIN:

No, it's not Titania.

OBERON: (indulgently)

You, villainous boy?

ROBIN:

Me, noble father!

OBERON: (standing)

Bad seed!

ROBIN:

It's only from you,
My lord, the good seed comes,
And I am honored to be yours.

OBERON: (stroking his hand)

That's nice. See here gentle prowler
What tale are you actually going to tell me
This morning?

ROBIN:

Eh! Still the same or as much as needed.

OBERON:

You are going to speak to me of my wife?

ROBIN:

Precisely.

OBERON:

What's that very changeable lady doing?

ROBIN:

She's hunting. And for a long while
Has never hunted better
Than last night: Rare game,
An inestimable booty,
A poet. Thus, this morning
You will be at once
Royally deceived.

OBERON:

I've done my share of that, lad.

ROBIN:

You, cheated on! Just like a man—
And you suffer it?

OBERON:

What do you want?
It's the essence
Of our immortal existence.
How can you expect fidelity
In the whole of eternity?

ROBIN:

Meanwhile, they're laughing at you.

OBERON: (getting excited)

Who is?

ROBIN:

Everyone, I tell you. Heaven and Earth!
When you pass through the clearing
The breeze chuckles in the birches
The rushes confide to the streams
Your conjugal misfortunes.
When the Queen takes a lover
Her name's like a drum
Sounding your ruin.
And the cricketing of crickets
And the comic baying of dogs
All tell you that your treasure is stolen.
And you hear nothing of it!
And the Moon gives you horns.
Father it is beyond all bounds.

OBERON:

Robin, you are making fun of me!
But your jesting is useful.
It arouses my bile;
So much so and in such a way
That I am going to make a shocking example!
Where are they? Speak!

ROBIN:

Titania is bringing
Yaun the Rhymer, and their approach is near.

OBERON:

Let's distance ourselves. Let's surprise them.

ROBIN:

Surprise them.

OBERON:

Thanks, Robin.

(aside)

As for her, my word, I love her enough, still.
It's crazy, but that's the way it is
I love her enough that her penance
Will merely be to forfeit the audacious one.
As for him, let him suffer in his soul
Let him suffer in his flesh! Let him die
Disenchanted, despairing.

(to Robin)

Son, you are going to see how I avenge myself.
They're laughing at me? That's fine.

They are going to weep.

INVISIBLE VOICES:

When you pass through the clearing
The breeze is in the birches
The rushes are telling the roses
Of your conjugal misfortunes.

(The symphony continues after the chorus. It is caressingly
sensual. Titania and Yaun appear, tenderly entwined.)

TITANIA:

Yaun! It's here in this marvelous land
This land of vermillion splendors,
It's here that I can love you.

YAUN:

In our aerial wanderings
I saw snowy mountains pass
And huge silent forests.
I saw cities disappear.
Where are we?

TITANIA:

Here you are going to know
Inexhaustible sensuality.

YAUN:

Dream! Passionate reality
Is it true that I possess you?

TITANIA:

I am yours.

YAUN:

Your arms, your lips!
All your sweet and changing being,
I adore you! Queen, let's love each other!

TITANIA:

To appease, to reignite our fevers
Centuries of love will be ours.
You will taste inexpressible ecstasy.

YAUN:

And at your knees I will forget the Earth.

TITANIA:

You will sing in poetic phrase
Of a joy that one can die of,
If I do not give you imperishable youth.

YAUN: (transported)

Yes, imperishable youth
At your side! Distant from you, death!
Ideal beauty! Triumphant chimera!

TITANIA:

Ah! I see how powerful your love is!

YAUN:

I adore you—your arms, your lips!
Your whole being is charming and sweet.
Let's love each other.

TITANIA:

Let's love each other.

(They keep embracing. Suddenly, Titania pulls loose from
Yaun's grip, looks about and listens, worried.)

TITANIA:

Silence!
The bird is fleeing in the immense azure
The ether shivers. From these sure signs
I foretell the coming of Oberon, my spouse.
He must not see you.
On your eyes let me twice rest my lips.

Yaun, sleep now.
Around him, rise white clouds
To hide him from Oberon's gaze.
Sleep child, sleep, until the promised hour
When my kisses will awaken you.

(As she speaks, she takes Yaun's hand; Yaun was kneeling before her. She kisses his eyes twice and he falls gently off to sleep. As Titania completes her enchantment clouds grow around Yaun and conceal him. Oberon appears. Robin, following him, distances himself, laughing as he leaves.)

OBERON: (not without irony)

Titania, my queen, was awaiting me.

TITANIA:

I'm always expecting you.

OBERON:

Without impatience.

TITANIA:

What do you mean, king?

OBERON:

For more than three nights
The passion of the hunt has enthralled you,
Queen, have you actually coursed through woods and
plains?

TITANIA:

What's it to you? I act according to my whim.

OBERON:

Your arrow has brought down hinds and roe
What's more, they say that by your charms was captured
A poet, an even more important conquest.
Show him to me!

TITANIA:

You are laughing?

OBERON:

Sometimes I joke.
But not today, mad Titania.
Know that I'm being laughed at in my kingdom.
That's enough.

TITANIA:

Oberon jealous?
Like a mortal, like a banal spouse!
I was right, you're laughing.

OBERON: (imperiously)

Will you show me this man?

TITANIA: (aggressively)

In that case, show me your Philida
Who's succeeded so many others.
We are even, go, my flighty Oberon.

OBERON:

I am your master!

TITANIA:

And I, what am I, the eternal woman
Free with my love? I give its flower
To whoever pleases me, according to my heart's inclination.
Beautiful, I return to you. What more do you want?

OBERON:

I want your obedience

And your respect. In my immense realm
They've been jesting over my kindness a bit too long.
That's over. Henceforth you will be condemned
To blind fidelity.
That'll be a change for you.

TITANIA:

You'll change yourself?

OBERON:

Ah, don't irritate me! Your poet—

TITANIA:

I love him.

OBERON:

You love him? You'll kick him out;
You'll send him back to Earth
To common humanity.
Obey!

TITANIA:

Oberon, I'll brave
Your will that wants to enslave me.

OBERON:

Thank my love, which still remains to you.
Obey!

TITANIA:

No!

OBERON: (pointing to where Yaun is hidden)

That's where he's sleeping.
I shan't disturb his dreams.
But may all crumble about him,
May all the foliation wither
May all the shining flowers fade,
May Winter succeed Spring.
Let him awake in a frozen forest,
In his disturbed thoughts
In his unsatiated desire.
And let him not see your arms open to him except to ruin
    him
 And to despair forever!

VOICES IN SPACE: (with subterranean growls)

Forever! Forever!

TITANIA: (raging)

Cursed be your power!

Cursed, thrice cursed!

(she leaves)

OBERON: (laughing)

Go, you can curse me
And now, forest, laugh if you like to laugh!

CURTAIN

ACT III

IN THE FOREST

AT RISE, Yaun appears dozing under the oak of the fairies in the forest where he was seen for the first time. Near Yaun is Hermine, filled with anguish, trying to make him come to.

HERMINE:

Is he dead! In this glacial forest
He remained all night!
Yaun, come to! Speak to me! I am succumbing.

YAUN: (coming to, weakly)

Titania!

HERMINE:

Whose name are you uttering?

YAUN: (standing up)

Titania!

HERMINE:

I'm the one who's answering you!

YAUN:

Hermine!

HERMINE:

During the whole night your companions
Vainly sought you. What's become of you?
Your face is burning, your hands are icy,
You are trembling. Get up.

YAUN:

If that's the case, alas! Nothing is real
I only had a dream.
No, I didn't hold the adored in my arms,
I didn't possess her.
Brutally, I'm falling from heaven

HERMINE:

Lean your weak hand on my arm.

YAUN: (distracted)

Who's speaking? Ah, yes, it's you,
Hermine!

HERMINE:

Friend, in a nearby house
The first fire of the season is lit
Come! In your heart, a calm day
Will reflower with divine hope.

YAUN: (seeing her at last)

Sis, why come back?
Go toward joy and youth.
Leave me alone.

HERMINE:

Poor friend, remember
I swore to dedicate my life to you.
Tenderly, humbly.
I know how to keep my oath.

YAUN:

Hermine, your sweetness is a constant reproach to me.
Ah! Your pure love ought to deserve love

HERMINE:

And you cannot love!

YAUN:

Because I cannot live
I wanted to possess the ideal.

HERMINE:

I wanted
To live with your dream and your sorrow.

YAUN:

Hermine. I am no longer waiting
Even for my dream.
And I am dying of this torture
Of believing even for a single moment
In the ungraspable chimera.
And I'm cowardly, you plainly see—
Yes, I'm a coward and a wretch
Not to dare to break this chain
Which makes my thought captive
And from my poor soul, to tear out
The cruel arrow that wounded it.

HERMINE:

And as for me, I dream in terror

That I will be nothing without you.
That your glance is my light
That if I must not see you
Everything in heaven will be black
And death will be dear to me!

YAUN:

Death! That's the supreme hope
For those who cannot live their dream!

HERMINE:

Death is the dawn that rises
In the gaze of those in despair.
If you want to die, I will die.

YAUN:

I will die of this illness
Of knowing heaven is closed to me.

HERMINE:

I will die for having loved you.
If, poet, you would yet
Forget your mad dream
The future will be a ball
Which will disguise the past from us.
To allow me, at last, to love you.
You will experience some sweetness.

While knitting white wool
I will listen to your beautiful poems
And I'll warm up your heart next to mine.
Yaun, I belong to you.

YAUN:

No, Hermine, no. I don't love you.
My life is finished.
I want to leave this Earth,
To go down there, to the unknown
Into the mystery
To the land of eternal rest
Goodbye, Hermine, and forever.

HERMINE:

The end! Ah! I implore it!

YAUN:

Death—that's the supreme hope.
For he who cannot live his dream.

HERMINE:

Death—it's the dawn rising
To the gaze of the desperate.

YAUN:

So let it be!

HERMINE:

If you die, I will die!

(Snow begins to fall. Titania appears. Behind her, less distinct, appears the fairy paradise.)

YAUN: (in ecstasy)

Titania! I see—

TITANIA: (with a distant voice)

"Woman, ever beautiful in her youthful splendor
Heart still passionate with a superb flame
None of the miseries of the flesh
Ideal tenderness and intoxication."

HERMINE: (turning towards Yaun and seeing only him.)

Your face is clearing up!
You are smiling! You love me!

VOICES IN SPACE:

O chimeras!
Illusions of impossible loves!

THE STENDHAL HAMLET SCENARIOS, ED. BY FRANK J. MORLOCK * 109

Final reflections of vain hopes.

YAUN, HERMINE, TITANIA:

Let's be off to the land of ecstasy!
Spirits of heaven surround us!
Travel on shining wings.
Carry us away, forever united
Into infinite space!

OBERON: (appearing) (sneering)

No! fools— Night. The unreachable end
Your dreams are over!

(In a roll of thunder, the luminous vision fades. With a great shout of despair Yaun and Hermine fall. Snow covers the bodies of Yaun and Hermine. White solitude. The shepherd Mathias passes under the trees, striding with a hurried step, supported by his staff, wallet on his back, droning out a song.)

MATHIAS: (alone)

Harsh days are come.
Hard for the poor.
White sheep, horned rams
Return to the stable.
To the gold of bearded oaks
Is mixed the silvery snow.
Winter besieges us.

Harsh days are come.
Sadness and coldness.
With thrushes and lilies,
Sleep shrouded lovers!
Nothing lasts.

CURTAIN

OBERON'S HORN

by

Georges Ephraim Mikhael

1888

CAST OF CHARACTERS

TITANIA

ORIANA

SILVÈRE

OBERON

OBERON'S HORN

The stage represents clearing in a forest of the fairies. Among the luminescent grass and flowers flows a fountain. To the right rose bushes. Titania is seated near the fountain. She is dividing on her spinning wheel fine threads made from the rays of the moon.

TITANIA:

O resplendent threads, o thread the color of stars,
Will you be the mantle of a prince or indeed the veil
Of a queen? No, no, thread the color of spring,
I intend that you be the floating curtains of lightning
Used on the passionate bed of a woman in love
Like a pavilion of gold on a lucky barge.

(A silence, the spinning wheel stops, Titania lets her spindle drop and dreams)

Yes, as for me, the calm sister of lilies and branches,
I love to love, and it's my customary pleasure
To go to sleep a virgin and with dreams of a spouse.
O nuptial dreams,

(excitedly, reproaching herself)

Well, am I jealous?
Titania will be jealous of lovers?
Ah! Madwoman! Don't I have in my sleeping palace
The pride of ineffably pure sensuality?
Down there, in the blue bushes, I pluck instead of mulber-
    ries,
Sapphires, and at night, in turning my spindle,
I hear mandrakes singing. My birds
Exhale in their flight a perfume of corollas
And I am a fairy and I know the words
Which make unknown stars rise up in heaven.
I can do anything.

(sadly)

No! because my long hair, my naked arms,
My throat which throbs under my bestarred dress
None see them; and if sometimes in an alley
A traveler struck by the heavens and the forests
Passes by singing in the distance: quick, I disappear!
Because Oberon, king of enchanted forests
Wishes it so! I can sleep under the oaks
By the road. The passerby won't be dazzled,
To awaken me: I am invisible for him,
And everywhere, I mix myself into the vapors of paths,
With the mists of the moon, with the shivering brilliance
Which expires over fields, gardens and woods.

(she admires herself in the fountain)

Alas! For whom am I beautiful? Why heaven,
You see me where eyes waken, and you, living forest,
You see me. The kiss that my dream boasts of,
The kiss is not worth the caress of evening,
Perfumed totally with fairy flowers. My power
Is much sweeter than love. I am the happy queen
Who's never been troubled by any desire.

ORIANA: (entering abruptly)

Godmother!
Avenge me!

TITANIA:

Oriana! Oh! How enraged your eyes are!

ORIANA:

Listen to me! Formerly, amongst the rose bushes
You found me like a bee exiled
From beautiful gold hives.

TITANIA: (laughing)

And I stole you.

ORIANA:

You took me in your arms, godmother, and I grew
As the forest gilds a magic noon.

TITANIA:

Yes, but sometimes you flee the divine light.
You go away, deploying, o my sweet warrior,
Your hair like a noble standard in the wind
And I know that down there you often triumph
And that in proud evenings you choose for an escort
Sad kings that you tame.

ORIANA:

Yes, I am strong!
My feet repose on great shields
Like frail and familiar white birds
Battling on the high roofs of citadels.
Yes, everywhere unknown and faithful lovers
Are waiting for me. Well, there, in the woods, this morn-
    ing
I don't know what puerile and loud singer
Was insulting me, do you understand, me the victorious!
But you will avenge me.

TITANIA:

My beautiful fury,
Tell me what the insult was?

ORIANA:

I was wandering,
Listening vaguely under the cool foliage

To the friendly murmurs of a sacred spring.
Suddenly (surely, I must have been wrong), my golden
    belt
And my dress I had thrown in the bushes
And smiling with shivering shyness
I hid myself in the splendor of the fountain.

TITANIA: (excitedly)

And the child who was dreaming on the distant path
Ran, saw the shining light of your hair,
Intoxicated himself on your flesh and in his nervous arms
Seized, like a shield, conqueror of a faun,
Your dear body bursting with royal youth?

ORIANA: (a bit confused)

Eh! No, it wasn't like that.

TITANIA:

You were telling me
Of an insult?

ORIANA:

Alas! while I veiled
My face with my half closed hands, the savage child,
Without hiding amongst the willows of the river bank,
Without espying the fountain in which I was still laughing,
Passed his eyes to heaven, disdainfully singing.

TITANIA:

Surely, granddaughter, he gravely offended you.
He's going to die, that's agreed.

ORIANA:

I wasn't thinking
Of killing him! You see this foreign child,
I hate him. But you can hate without butchery.
And I wasn't dreaming of the unique pleasure
Of seeing him devoured by wolves and hounds.

TITANIA:

Do you want him to love you?

ORIANA:

No! It's too late for that. Truly,
I don't know what I want. Imagine a torture.

(she thinks)

To enchain him on the terrifying shore of a gulf?
No! Change him into a stone, into a tree? He's got to suf-
    fer
And the rock feels nothing, and trees have too many flow-
    ers.
Let's keep looking! The earth is impoverished by sorrows!
Wait! Near the spring where I was offended

Let him be troubled by some strange fiancée
So that I will hear mounting to the deaf and distant heav-
ens
His tears and screams of vain amours.

TITANIA:

By whom will we make him punished?

(abruptly, to herself)

Oh! What an idea.

(To Oriana)

The punishment is certain, because you will be helped
By someone very great.

ORIANA:

Heavens! Have I guessed?
It's you who are going to—

TITANIA:

Why that astonished look?
I am obeying you. I want to punish him myself.

ORIANA:

Consider. So he will scream to you "I love you."

And leaning towards your lips he'll whisper
Conquering words. You won't weaken?

TITANIA:

Titania can never soften.

ORIANA:

Are you sure?

TITANIA:

Yes, my sovereign heart doesn't fear wounding
By vain amours.

ORIANA: (resigned)

So be it! If you want to, avenge me!

(Titania comes forward toward the trees and makes magic
passes with her spindle.)

TITANIA:

Oberon, Oberon, I'm calling you, o my king!

OBERON: (appearing)

What do you want now? Are you going to ask me again
For a dress soaked in the whirlpool of the dawn?

Do you want to drink the light of the moon? Must
Some one weave you a veil from April mist?
To decorate your face and ears
Must I bring to summer nights vermilion stars?

TITANIA:

No, neither jewels from heaven nor dress! My wish
Is to be no longer alone in the mute woods.
King, I intend that a young, mincing man wait
To speak to me sensuously and smile at me.
Release this cruel oath that forbids me
To appear. I want for a child down there
To see in the eternal night of the world
My resplendent throat like a blonde ray.
I intend to deliver my hair to the terrestrial wind.

OBERON:

You want to be a woman, Titania! These prayers
Are unworthy of you! What! You're a fairy.
You spend the night, luminous and dressed
With rays; you gather all the flowers from heaven.
You plunder, like a child thief with honey
The wave filled with savory light!
And then, alas, you want to be, some impassioned lover
Some girl furtively prowling the night
In the shadow of the highways, in the arms of her lover.
And beware, o my innocent Titania,
Of hugging a rustic with a donkey's head!

TITANIA: (very grave)

No potion, o my king, has disturbed my reason.
Me, lose my dignity! No, I am from much too noble a
    house,
Being born, one spring, of an enchanted pearl.
But, sire, you haven't listened to me enough,
For I want to appear, one day only, one moment
To a pitiful child who's calling me with distraction
And weeping to see me. (supplicating) A single day! What
    do you care!
Since he will see me like a dead star
Swallowed by the sadness of the sea.
And his heart will keep like a bitter perfume
The mortal memory of my illusory lips.

OBERON:

Go! But keep this silver horn, pale and ivory.
If the child, captivated by your youthful splendor,
Disturbs your heart with a wicked passion,
If your face blushes with a carnal light,
Call me. If not, you will be exiled
Eternally. Forever, with vain sobs,
You will wail, woman, far from the divine palace.
But when you wish to flee the shame of the earth,
No matter where you may be, in a solitary valley,
In tumultuous fields, in dozing woods,
Blow with the ivory horn towards friendly stars.
I will come to get you like a rich spoil
Towards the country of dreams and fairy joy.

(Oberon disappears.)

TITANIA:

Oriana! I am delightfully frightened.
Woman! I have annoying hail beneath my feet,
Cool grass, I who flew naked,
Now I feel as if I were naked,
And as if the evening wind were closer
To my face. O new smell of forests.
Formerly, in my divine courses, I aspirated
I don't know what magic perfumes. The water of fountains
Is changing between my lips into a celestial liquor.
How good the water of fountains is! All my heart
Shivers when the rude wind grazes my shoulders!
Oh! I want to run down there amongst the willows
But it's time. You see how I will avenge you.
Let's find this insolent.

ORIANA:

Ah! I would have preferred
Less zeal!

(Titania gestures in surprise)

Don't you go believing that I love him,
This prowler of forests, pale and harmonious.
He's a dreamer, a fool who chats with the wind
And walks through shivering flowers, drinking
The idle sensuality of the easterly breeze.

At least you won't be a rival.
Surely, he will touch you with his human desires.
If his lip offers insult to your snowy hands,
You will sound your horn and you will ruin everything
In the fogs of this native sky.

TITANIA: (impatiently)

Eh! Yes, no question.
Let's go towards this child.

(A hunting flute in the distance, than a raised voice.)

ORIANA:

He's here. I hear His songs.

TITANIA:

Yes, down there, indecisive and floating
With murmurs of flute awakening closed flowers.
Let's spy on him. Come let's hide ourselves among these
    roses.

SILVÈRE: (in the distance)

Girls dancing in the vines
On the dark and charming lake
Listening to the swans' bye byes
Expiring melodiously.
Dancing choirs of wine-picking girls

Joining around the wine press
Listening to dreaming voices
Of swans dying in the night.

(he appears at the edge of the woods)

Yes, the swans! The white songbirds! I envy them
And I'd like to die the way they do, soul ravished,
Singing nobly on beloved streams.
O music! Woods with perfumed orchards,
A potent song escapes, intoxicating me.
Down there, folks told me, one day you may live
Without hearing the triumphant noise of trees.
But, be certain, they were mocking me. It's false.
Because, as for me, I know for sure, to live you must
Mix your voice with the gay or plaintive sound
Of the good forest, with breezes, with streams.
O my god! I would like to be all the birds.

(listens to a nightingale singing)

Nightingale. He's going away! The beasts are naughty!

(turning towards the trees, hands joined as if praying to the
nightingale)

I'd so much like to know the song you're singing!

(Silvère leans back against the tree as in ecstasy. Titania
half emerges from the bushes and gestures to Oriana to
remain hidden.)

TITANIA:

Languishing night! Distant odor of hay,
Ecstasy! Ah! I am mad! It's time. Let's punish
The insulter!

(turning towards Silvère)

Heavens! He's asleep. A sorceress
Has touched him, perhaps, or a gypsy
Poured over his eyes a vase of sleepiness.
What's he doing there, standing up?

(to Silvère)

Why, you are like
Birds dozing in branches. No question
You aren't listening to me!

SILVÈRE: (without turning)

I'm not sleeping, I am listening.
Begone. The peaceful night was so sweet.

TITANIA:

Rude! No, I intend to seat myself near you,
Quite near, to disturb you.

(Titania bursts into laughter. Silvère turns, astonished.)

SILVÈRE:

My God, am I in a delirium?
What marvelous bird was singing?

TITANIA:

That's my laugh!

SILVÈRE:

Oh! Mercy, laugh again!

TITANIA:

You want
To be alone in the happy shadow of thickets;
Make the woods laugh. I'm leaving.

SILVÈRE: (supplicating)

I beg you,
The two of us will watch in the ornate forest.
Stay! You must know mysterious tunes.
Just now I was naughty. How bright
Your eyes are!

(picking a flower, as Titania sits on a sort of bench covered with moss, she plays with the horn she holds in her hand)

Take this flower, it's a primrose.
This other one too.

TITANIA: (taking the flowers)

What's your name?

SILVÈRE:

Silvère!

TITANIA:

And what do you do?

SILVÈRE:

I sing with shepherds.
Here, these flowers, too! Put these light lilies
There, in the horn, just like in a white vase.
I know the whole woods. I know where the periwinkle
Hides and I know which tree is going to flower.
Would you like some hawthorn? Oh! I would like to offer
   you
The whole Springtime! Still. I'm afraid of you. You are
Very beautiful!

TITANIA: (coquettishly)

You think so!

SILVÈRE:

Yes, I've seen in fests,
Among kings dressed in silver and satin,
A joyous queen with a babyish smile
But your hand is more royal than hers.

TITANIA:

Truly?

SILVÈRE:

And your voice, blonde musician
Has the air of commanding these obedient woods.
Come closer, amongst the lilies. Oh! I feel I'm
Fainting delightfully.

(Silvère keeps gathering flowers; he brings them to Titania. Titania keeps playing with the horn in which he places flowers as in a vase. When Silvère turns toward her, she nonchalantly places the horn on the mossy bench.)

SILVÈRE:

Stay close by like that.
I am dreaming that divine night is bending
Over me like a beautiful and serene sister.

ORIANA: (leaving the bushes)

Get out of here, he loves you enough.

TITANIA: (to Oriana)

Soon.

(to herself)

O sweet
Words of love!

SILVÈRE:

See, in your breath
I'm inhaling flowers taken from the plain.
Give me your lips.

TITANIA: (not protecting herself very well)

No! No!

ORIANA: (coming out of her bushes)

Isn't it time
Yet?

TITANIA: (as if in ecstasy)

Time?

ORIANA:

Come on, quick, the horn?

SILVÈRE:

Your blonde hair illuminates and perfumes
The sweet shadow and the evening veils with foggy light.

ORIANA:

Let's hurry up!

TITANIA: (to Oriana)

A minute more! Could you be afraid?

(laughing to herself)

I'm laughing
But my heart is trembling like a startled bird.

SILVÈRE: (rising, going toward her and hurling himself on her)

I love you!

ORIANA:

Will you blow that horn!

TITANIA:

So be it! My job's finished.

(with an affected irony, she frees herself)

Goodnight, child! Yes, from irony I allowed
Your young lips to wander on my scattered hair
And I was laughing with you. But that's enough, I'm leav-
     ing.

(going toward the bench and picking up the horn)

SILVÈRE:

You're leaving! O my God, you are leaving me. I'm trem-
     bling.
What have I done? Stay! Why it seems to me
Since you are fleeing me that the summer moon
Is withdrawing to heaven and taking back its light.
It seems to me that the forests are desolated
That you are going to carry them off like stolen flowers
In your dress, and with them all the stars of heaven in your
     hands.
O I am suffering from love.

(Silvère weeps, head in hands. Titania puts the horn back
on the bench.)

TITANIA: (dreaming)

A delicious thought
Spreading over me again!

SILVÈRE:

You've taken my calm evenings from me,
You've taken the forests and the palm gardens,
You've taken the fraternal friendship of the birds from me.
I will sing no more: eternal sobs
Will choke my beloved songs in me.
When I am walking under the sad branches
I will no longer know the caress of the woods
And my exiled heart will no longer hear its voice.

(Titania pretends to be looking ironically at him)

O I will die from your scornful glance!

TITANIA:

Well, no! I lied! You know, o breeze,
O luminous and blond footpath that I walked through,
And you, clear, friendly fountain yes, you will know him,
You towards whom I incline my aerial glory,
I can no longer leave now. I am his.

SILVÈRE:

What are you saying?

TITANIA:

Take me, Silvère, I consent.

SILVÈRE:

Come! I am going to carry you off in my trembling arms
Across the splendor of the guilty forest.
So that the marriage of our two dreams shall be accomplished
The nuptial stars are closing their clement eyes.
In all the woods for the success of lovers
A fairy springtime weighs on the foliage.
Everything is silent. Not even the cry of an awakened little bird,
Not a shiver of wind on the calm lawn.
Come! Down there, I think I see heaven on the horizon
Opening for us a divine door.
Come! We are going to go into a fine ravine
And during our first embrace, we will feel
The indulgent roses leaning over our heads.

TITANIA:

Yes, love's intoxication disturbs my ardent soul
Let's flee!

ORIANA: (leaving the bushes)

Are you going to blow that horn! She's fleeing. Reckless!
You are avenging me too well, Titania! Thanks.

I didn't dream of punishing him like this.
Titania, Titania! Alas in the bushes—

(she looks in the thicket)

She weakened! The flowers are shaking around her,
Her undone hair seems like a stream of gold.
Oh! I intend to save her. I'm going to take the horn
Myself!

(she grabs the horn and puts it to her lips, the horn makes
no sound)

Prodigy! The horn remains mute!
Why, no—it's just these flowers. Get out, I tell you.
Nasty flowers!

(she tears the flowers out violently)

Finally, my resounding calls
Are going to evoke the savior king.

(she is about to blow when she takes a last look in the
bushes)

Too late!

(Titania and Silvère appear in the midst of the trees.)

TITANIA:

I prefer you to the king of magic glades.
I am a woman and, fleeing nostalgic dreams
In your arms, I will forget the joyous byways,
The divine shade and superhuman silences.
When kisses join our impassioned lips
Terrestrial love is the sweetest of fairies.

CURTAIN

THE FRENCH LEAR

or,

THE BEGGAR KING

(Anonymous)

(no date)

CAST OF CHARACTERS

The KING

HIS ELDEST DAUGHTER

HER HUSBAND

HIS YOUNGER DAUGHTER

THE GRANDCHILDREN OF THE KING

PASSERS BY

THE PUBLIC CRIER

ACT I

The old king is seated on his throne surrounded by his two daughters, their husbands and their children, along with his councilors and his guards.

KING: Approach, my daughters. And you, too, my sons-in-law, heroes without reproach to whom I confided them. My daughters, and you, also, my sons-in-law, who have become my sons, and you, also, my little grandchildren.

Approach, my eldest daughter, and your husband and your children. I will give you on the spot a great joy. God has given me the greatest joys in the world. I am glorious. I've conquered a vast empire. From the vaults of my palace hang the banners of my conquering armies. I am dreaded by my humiliated neighbors who no longer dare to bear arms against me. I am proud. Pride is not stupid vanity. Pride is satisfaction in having acted well. I am loved by my people. I am rich. I am happy. But, I am old. In new times, there must be new men. At my age there is no longer any hope. There remains only the pleasure of bringing joy to one's children. At my age one aims at repose in life while awaiting the repose of death. My daughters, I am going to share my empire between you two. There will be an Empress for the Empire of the North, and an Emperor for the Empire of the North, in other words, you, the eldest, and your husband. So also there will be an Empress for the Empire of the South and an Emperor for the Empire of the South, in other words, you, the youngest, and your husband. But, before initiating this solemn partition, I wish, my daughters, to know how you love me. You, the eldest, speak first.

ELDEST DAUGHTER: My father, your words would astonish others, but not me. For I know you to be as generous as you are glorious. And I understand that you aspire to rest after all your exploits. You have, indeed, deserved this rest. Your succession will be in good hands.

KING: Very good! You know me generous, it's true. But, that doesn't tell me how much you love me.

ELDEST DAUGHTER: Is it possible not to love someone who is generous?

KING: Agreed. But, how much do you love me?

ELDEST DAUGHTER: As one ought to love her father.

KING: Meaning—?

ELDEST DAUGHTER: Meaning, placing him higher in her heart than all other beings in the world.

KING: Even higher than her husband?

ELDEST DAUGHTER: Even higher than her husband. Didn't our father give us life?

KING: You hear, my son-in-law?

SON IN LAW: I hear, I hear. (aside) What you must endure when you want an empire!

KING: Continue, my daughter.

ELDEST DAUGHTER: Father, I love you as the greatest gift God can give to man. I love you like the Sun which warms the Earth, like the stars which light the night. I love you like the pure sky of Summer. I love you like the freshness of fountains in torrid days. I love you like flowers whose hardy perfume penetrates all that surrounds them.

KING: That's a good daughter who will raise my grandchildren in respect of my memory.

ELDEST DAUGHTER: I love you like hope. I love you like charity. I love you like goodness. I love you like justice.

KING: Stop! You have spoken well. You will be Empress of the Empire of the North and your husband will be Emperor. Now, my younger daughter, I am listening to you, and after the words of your sister, I ask myself, from curiosity, how you can say better!

YOUNGEST DAUGHTER: You know very well, my father, that it is not possible to find more eloquent and beautiful comparisons than those my sister has spoken. I could repeat her words.

KING: Do that then, since you cannot speak better of your father.

YOUNGEST DAUGHTER: Sire, our master, you want to share your realm. You say you are old; but age is not a sin, age is experience.

KING: Right! Right! But that is not the question.

YOUNGEST DAUGHTER: I beg your pardon, Sire, our master. Your hands are not debilitated, and our hands are less steady than yours. If, by the greatest of misfortunes, death took you from your people, we would do our best to be a worthy replacement for you. But, as long as you live, we ought to continue our apprenticeship, observing your example.

KING: If I understand you correctly, you think I'm going down the wrong path and you do not admire my generosity?

YOUNGEST DAUGHTER: I admire it, but I'm astounded by it. I have such confidence in you that I fear for your people the consequences of the rest you desire.

KING: I thank you much for that confidence, but nothing

in your speech tells me you love me.

YOUNGEST DAUGHTER: I love you as one ought to love her father.

KING: That's the first thing your sister said. Continue.

YOUNGEST DAUGHTER: What more is there to say?

KING: Pay close attention to your answers. Do you love me more than your husband?

YOUNGEST DAUGHTER: Not more. Differently.

KING: Weigh your words carefully. Which of us, me or your husband would you prefer to see die first?

YOUNGEST DAUGHTER: Neither the one nor the other! I've never thought of that. It would break my heart.

KING: Youngest daughter, don't put me in a passion! Consider you are risking a realm.

YOUNGEST DAUGHTER: Sire, our master, my sister said she loves you like justice. I have enough confidence in your justice to believe you will approve my frankness.

KING: My child, there is still time. Don't try my patience. I don't like quibbling. I don't like it when you evade answering a precise question, and hide it behind a seeming frankness which is nothing but hypocrisy. I'd really like to forget your strange attitude. Repeat word for word what your sister said to me. Come, my child, how much do you love me?

YOUNGEST DAUGHTER: Sire, our master, I love you like salt.

KING: What?

YOUNGEST DAUGHTER: Like salt—

KING: All you present here, listen carefully to my will. There will be no empire of the North, there will be no empire of the South. There will only remain my empire which I bestow on my eldest daughter. My eldest daughter loves me, my youngest daughter hates me. Ah, my eldest daughter, I beg your pardon. I preferred your sister. What a mistake! In giving you my empire I correct a terrible mistake. And you, the younger, pack your bags immediately, with your husband that you prefer to me, and your children. Under careful guard, you will be escorted outside the borders of the realm. I drive you out and I renounce you. And I am going to rest my old age amongst those who love me. I have spoken.

CURTAIN

ACT II

A year later, the king is living with his eldest daughter, who possesses the kingdom. The king is going down a corridor when he meets the Queen, followed by her guards. He tries to flee. The Queen has him seized by her guards.

QUEEN: Father, your attitude is intolerable. You pretend to be a victim. You take on the airs of a martyr.

KING: Daughter, I take on the airs of a man who is the victim of ingratitude. I have given you everything and you refuse me signs of respect before the entire court.

QUEEN: Why do you expect to be respected? You spend your time in the kitchens with the servants.

KING: That's because they've kept their friendship for me. To them, I am still the old king.

QUEEN: Aren't you ashamed to lack dignity to this degree? What can the court think when the Queen's father frequents the kitchen waiters?

KING: Possibly the Court thinks the Queen's father is not happy in his daughter's home!

QUEEN: In the days of your power, you wouldn't let anyone teach you a lesson. My sister knew something!

KING: What? You reproach me today for having despoiled your sister for you?

QUEEN: I've inherited your character and I won't tolerate anyone teaching me a lesson. You are an embarrassment here. This very day you will withdraw to a remote place, in the company of two or three servants you can share a drink with at the inns; if such is your good pleasure as fallen king.

KING: No, child without bowels! I do not accept your gift. It sticks to my body like the resin from a poisoned tree. From now on I shall make no scandal in your court. I am going to take the stick of a mendicant. And I will be a scandal throughout the whole world, which is larger than your court. And all will know how you've treated me. May your children one day renounce their mother, as you have renounced your father, daughter without bowels!

CURTAIN

ACT III

The wretched king wanders alone on the highway.

KING: Have pity on a man who has known happiness, who has known riches, who has known power!! A man is, indeed, more wretched who has fallen into misery after having been rich, than if he had been poor from birth. You who pass by, don't you recognize me? Don't you recognize your king? Give alms to your king if you please! Oh! Why do you go on your way shrugging your shoulders?

PEOPLE PASSING BY: He's a lunatic. Don't listen to him. Sometimes lunatics become dangerous!

KING: Why, no! I won't become dangerous, my friends! Dangerous men don't beg! See, I hold out my hand!

PEOPLE PASSING BY: If you have to give money to all the beggars on the highway, you won't have wherewith to pay for the inn when you get to town.

KING: I'm hungry, my friends.

PEOPLE PASSING BY: Pretend you are eating! That will appease your hunger.

KING: I am thirsty, my friends.

PEOPLE PASSING BY: It's going to rain! That will swell the streams! You will be able to drink!

KING: Formerly, you acclaimed me! Your voices drowned out the trumpets. You prostrated yourselves on my passing. Today, you'd let me die, mocking me.

PEOPLE PASSING BY: He's got delusions of grandeur. He thinks they respected him. He thinks they acclaimed him. Soon, he'll think he's Charlemagne.

(laughing, they leave)

KING: Oh! They're gone! In the past I never knew that the highways of my realm were so deserted, so icy. I didn't know that the people of my kingdom had such hard hearts. Alas, men scorn the poor. Alas, men only respect the rich. These people who refused me alms would have been neither richer nor poorer for having thrown me small crumbs. Alas, day is waning. Is it possible that I must stay alone on the road with all the phantoms that walk in the night? Ah! I'm afraid of solitude! I'm afraid death will come to meet me. He, who, in his old age, is surrounded by his children, and grand children laughs at death. He looks it in the face and yells at it, "You can carry me off but my lineage will go on through centuries." How cold it is on the road where there is no posterity. Only a poor shed, I cannot stand any more. If they repulse me at this cabin, I have only an hour to live. There's a young woman and children in the door way. I hear a woodcutter cutting wood. I am going to speak to this woman.—

You are poor people, but perhaps you will take pity on a wandering old man who is dying of hunger and can no longer put one foot before the other.

YOUNG WOMAN: Are you coming from far away?

KING: Oh, yes. From far away.

YOUNG WOMAN: We only have a little bread. Tomorrow my husband will cut another faggot, which he will try to sell, so you can eat a little. And you can rest.

KING: Thanks! You are better than my daughter.

YOUNG WOMAN: You have a bad daughter?

KING: Yes, very wicked.

YOUNG WOMAN: You say you came a long way? Have you crossed the Empire where they say the old king was driven out by his daughter?

KING: Are those your children who cling to your skirts?

YOUNG WOMAN: Yes. They've become fearful since

our misfortunes.

KING: You've had misfortunes?

YOUNG WOMAN: Great misfortunes.

KING: I am old; I am dirty; I have a long beard. Will you allow me to hug your children?

YOUNG WOMAN: Of course. Come in. Don't be afraid. Let this beggar hug you.

(The children come to him. The king kneels and embraces them.)

KING: My poor little children, forgive your old grandfather king who reduced you to misery. But God is just. I am as wretched as you.

YOUNGEST DAUGHTER: Father! What happiness! You will stay with us.

KING: Ah, my daughter, my favorite daughter. Why did you tell me you loved me like salt?

YOUNGEST DAUGHTER: Salt! Salt, father— Didn't you understand it is a blessing despite its bitter taste? What good would be the bread we eat if it didn't contain salt? It is indispensable to life, and I wanted to tell you I loved you like life.

KING: You've always been a little argumentative, my little girl.

CURTAIN

ACT IV

The Town Crier appears with drums and fanfares.

TOWN CRIER: I, the Town Crier, obedient to the orders of the King, tell you that the eldest daughter of the king, her husband and her children, have been exiled to a place where they are ordered to remain quietly. The Youngest Daughter of the King assumes the crown. The King hopes that his youngest daughter will be nicer to him than his eldest daughter. He has reason to believe it having seen that his youngest daughter always was very honest to him while the elder gave pretty speeches and he knows it, to his cost.— BE IT PROCLAIMED that the King advises his subjects not to be tightfisted when a beggar holds out his hand on the highway. Because no one knows with whom he may have to do, in the same way, nobody knows who is going to live and who is going to die.

CURTAIN

ABOUT FRANK J. MORLOCK

FRANK J. MORLOCK has written and translated many plays since retiring from the legal profession in 1992. His translations have also appeared on Project Gutenberg, the Alexandre Dumas Père web page, Literature in the Age of Napoléon, Infinite Artistries.com, and Munsey's (formerly Blackmask). In 2006 he received an award from the North American Jules Verne Society for his translations of Verne's plays. He lives and works in México.

www.ingramcontent.com/pod-product-compliance
Lightning Source LLC
LaVergne TN
LVHW091301080426
835510LV00007B/346